12 WOMEN IN BUSINESS

by Brianna L. DeVore

12 STORY LIBRARY
MORE TO EXPLORE

www.12StoryLibrary.com

12-Story Library is an imprint of Bookstaves.

Photographs ©: Diane Bondareff/Associated Press, cover, 1; Senado Federal/CC2.0, 4; José Reynaldo da Fonseca/CC3.0, 5; Sharaf Maksumov/Shutterstock.com, 5; Diane Bondareff/Associated Press, 6; John Gress Media Inc/Shutterstock.com, 7; Steve Lagreca/Shutterstock.com, 7; GPA Photo Archive/Xerox/CC2.0, 8; Yuri Gripas/dpa/Associated Press, 9; dennizn/Shutterstock.com, 9; PD, 10; EileenF/CC3.0, 11; Johnny Green/PA Images/Alamy, 12; pio3/Shutterstock.com, 12; Pear285/CC1.0, 13; Neja Hrovat/Shutterstock.com, 13; Sofia Negron/Science History Institute/CC3.0, 14; Withwi/CC3.0, 14; Science History Institute/YouTube, 15; Krista Kennell/Shutterstock.com, 16; PD, 17; Michael Vi/Shutterstock.com, 17; Stuart Isett/Fortune Most Powerful Women/CC2.0, 18; Belevich.Nastya/Shutterstock.com, 19; Kevin Anthony Carney/CC3.0, 20; Joseph St Pierre/CC3.0, 21; Stuart Isett/Fortune Most Powerful Women/CC2.0, 22; Darin Russell/US Air Force, 23; Associated Press, 24; The Rose of Sharon Foundation/YouTube, 25; PD, 26; darksoul72/Shutterstock.com, 26; That Hartford Guy/CC2.0, 27; Levi Clancy/CC4.0, 28; SDASM Archives/PD, 29

ISBN
9781632357748 (hardcover)
9781632358837 (paperback)
9781645820543 (ebook)

Library of Congress Control Number: 2019938626

Printed in the United States of America
September 2019

About the Cover
Mary Barra in 2017.

Access free, up-to-date content on this topic plus a full digital version of this book. Scan the QR code on page 31 or use your school's login at 12StoryLibrary.com.

Table of Contents

1

Luiza Helena Trajano: Growing the Family Business

When she was 12, Luiza Helena Trajano spent her school vacations working at her aunt's gift shop. Years later, she would turn that gift shop into a billion-dollar company.

Trajano was born in 1951 in the village of Franca, Brazil. Her aunt Luiza started a small store called Magazine Luiza in 1957. In Portuguese, Brazil's national language, "magazine" means store.

When Trajano turned 18, she started working in the store.

By 1991, she had worked in every department. Her aunt decided she was ready to take over. Trajano expanded the company into lots of new stores. She moved the corporate offices to São Paulo, a major city.

Trajano used unique promotions to increase sales. She created a program that allows customers to buy things on credit. They pay in small amounts over a long period of time. Magazine Luiza charges lower interest rates than credit card companies. This built customer loyalty. By 2017, Magazine Luiza had over 800 stores and around 23,000 employees. Trajano turned the company over to her son in 2016.

Luiza Helena Trajano in 2017.

A Magazine Luiza store in São Paulo.

24,000

Number of members in Luiza Trajano's Women of Brazil group

- Trajano created the group in 2013 with 40 female executives.
- Their goal is to create a Brazil that is better for all citizens.
- They offer job training for immigrants, free health care in schools, campaign promotion for women in politics, and other programs.

KNOWING YOUR CUSTOMER

In the early 2000s, Magazine Luiza wanted to move into e-commerce. But many of their customers were poor. The company built computer labs in rural areas. A specialist showed people how to use computers. Free internet use and online classes were made available. A digital showroom helped customers feel confident about buying something they couldn't see in person.

2

Mary Barra: Transforming an Industry

Mary Barra in 2017.

Mary Barra is the first woman in history to head a major US automobile company. She was born in Michigan in 1961. Her father worked for General Motors (GM). At 18, she signed up for a program at GM that helped pay her college tuition. She spent part of the year working for the company. Her first job was inspecting car hoods and fenders for mistakes. She spent the other part of the year in college.

Barra earned her degree in electrical engineering. For a time, she worked for GM as a senior engineer. Then GM paid for her to go to Stanford University to get her master's degree in business.

Returning to GM, Barra was successful in several management positions. She led a plant of 3,400 employees. She was put in charge of human resources. Starting in 2011, she headed the design and development of all GM vehicles.

In 2014, Barra was named Chief Executive Officer (CEO) of GM. Since becoming CEO, Barra has worked to position GM for the future. She bought a self-driving technology company. She started a car-sharing service. Barra is moving GM toward making more electric cars.

LOOKING TO THE FUTURE

In November 2018, GM decided to cut thousands of jobs and close several US plants. Barra received a lot of criticism for that decision. The economy was doing well. But Barra knew the plants would have to close eventually. She chose to close them while workers had a better chance of finding new jobs.

$2.6 billion+

Amount GM paid in fines for a bad part that caused the deaths of 124 people

- Barra found out about the part when she became CEO in 2014.
- She immediately told the National Highway Traffic Safety Administration.
- She fired 15 GM employees for knowing about the problem and not doing anything.

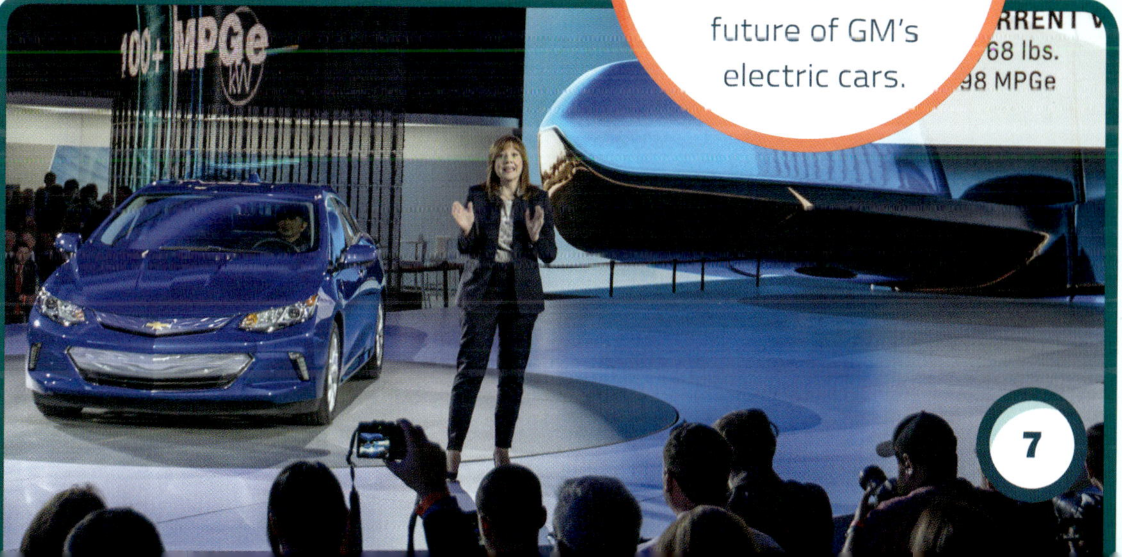

Barra speaks at the North American International Auto Show about the future of GM's electric cars.

3 Ursula Burns: A Leader for Women and Minorities

In 2009, Ursula Burns became the first African American woman to lead a Fortune 500 company. She was born in 1958 in New York City. She was raised by her mother in a poor neighborhood. Her mother worked odd jobs to send her to a good school. From her, Burns learned the importance of hard work and education.

In 1980, Burns received her degree in mechanical engineering. She had always been good at math. But she wasn't sure what kind of career she could have. Xerox, a document management and business services company, was offering to help interns pay for their degrees. Burns took advantage of this opportunity. She spent the next 36 years with Xerox.

Burns worked her way up through the company. By 1997, she had moved from executive assistant to vice president of worldwide manufacturing. She made the company money after it took on heavy losses in the early 2000s. Once she was made CEO, Burns helped move Xerox into the digital age.

In 2009, President Barack Obama asked Burns to help with his Science, Technology, Engineering, and Mathematics (STEM) Education Coalition. Helping women and minorities in STEM is still her passion.

Ursula Burns in 2015.

Burns with US President Barack Obama in 2013.

THE FORTUNE 500

Each year, the financial magazine *Fortune* publishes the Fortune 500. This is a list of 500 US companies that made the most money in sales. The list is based on sales numbers reported to the government. Companies on the list often use it to brag about their success.

1989

Year when Ursula Burns spoke up for herself at a company-wide event

- An executive was asked why the company hired women and minorities.
- Burns thought his answer didn't show enough support for women and minorities.
- The executive was impressed by Burns and helped further her career.

4

Kate Gleason: A Woman of Many Firsts

Catherine Anselm "Kate" Gleason is best known as an engineer. Her accomplishments as an entrepreneur, inventor, and banker are not as widely recognized today.

She was born in 1865 in Rochester, New York. Her father owned a toolmaking business. At 14, Gleason helped her father with bookkeeping. But she wanted to do more. She taught herself mechanics and engineering.

At 19, Gleason became the first woman to attend Cornell University's engineering program. She left school early to help her father's company. She quickly became head of bookkeeping and sales. At 27, she traveled overseas to grow the family business. Gleason Corporation was one of the first American companies to expand to Europe.

In 1917, Gleason was named head of the First National Bank of Rochester. She had no family ties to the bank. This was another first. During that time, she also started eight different businesses. She helped another machining

Kate Gleason and a bill with her signature on it.

Gleason's concrete houses are still lived in today.

company out of bankruptcy. A natural inventor, she designed one of the first known camper trailers. She was the first female member of the American Society of Mechanical Engineers.

Gleason spent much of her later life building communities. She started businesses and built affordable housing in New York, South Carolina, and California. She also restored a small community in France after it was bombed in World War I.

THINK ABOUT IT

Gleason is not in many history books today. Scholars say she was a visionary, like Steve Jobs of Apple. Why do you think she isn't better known?

100

Number of concrete homes Kate Gleason built in 1921 in Concrest, New York

- They were built to last. Some are still lived in today.
- Gleason designed the homes and oversaw construction, often calling workers by name.
- The six-room homes were sold for a small down payment and $40 a month. This was an affordable rate for working families at the time.

5 Anita Roddick: Beauty Products with a Mission

Anita Roddick in 2001.

Anita Roddick was born in England in 1942. Her parents were Italian immigrants. When she was 10, she saw pictures of World War II concentration camps. From that moment on, she cared about social justice. By 13, she was joining protests. Her dedication to social issues would help turn a small cosmetics store into a global empire.

In 1962, Roddick began traveling the world. She went to Tahiti, Australia, and South Africa. She enjoyed learning from local women. They shared their traditional ways of making self-care products, like lotions and shampoos.

She met her husband, Gordon Roddick, when she returned from her travels. After their daughters were born, Gordon took a long trip. Anita had to support the children on her own. In 1976, she opened The Body Shop. She created beauty products using knowledge gained in her travels. All were 100 percent natural and were not tested on animals.

Stories and photos explained each product.

Customers loved the products and the stories behind them. Most of Roddick's marketing was word-of-mouth. By 1991, The Body Shop had more than 2,000 stores in 50 countries. Under her leadership, many of the profits went to charity. Roddick herself started orphanages in Romania and co-founded a job program for homeless people. In 2003, Queen Elizabeth II appointed her a Dame Commander of the Order of the British Empire.

49,000

Number of people in Ghana helped by The Body Shop every year

- Since 1994, the Tungteiya Women's Association in Ghana has been selling shea butter to The Body Shop.
- The 18-step process to create shea butter has been passed down from mother to daughter for generations.
- The money earned goes toward improving health care, sanitation, water access, and education in their communities.

Women in Ghana packaging shea butter.

6

Kiran Mazumdar-Shaw: Bringing Medicine to the Poor

Kiran Mazumdar-Shaw is India's only female self-made billionaire. She was born to a middle-class family in Bangalore, India, in 1953. Her father brewed beer at India's largest brewery. He raised Mazumdar-Shaw as an equal to her brothers.

Mazumdar-Shaw wanted to be a doctor. But her grades weren't good enough. Her father encouraged her to brew beer. She went to Australia to study brewing. When she returned, she could not find a job. Breweries would not hire a woman.

In 1978, a businessman asked to form a partnership with her. She would use science to study fruit, and he would sell that science to food companies. Mazumdar-Shaw started her side of the business out of a garage. Known as Biocon, the company was a part of a new industry called biotechnology.

Kiran Mazumdar-Shaw in 2014.

Mazumdar-Shaw spent 20 years studying natural chemicals. She discovered a faster and cheaper way to make insulin. Insulin is a drug that helps

people with diabetes. Mazumdar-Shaw broke off from her business partner and made this Biocon's focus. She also started a company that performs scientific research for other companies.

In 2009, Mazumdar-Shaw started the Mazumdar-Shaw Cancer Center. The center offers free cancer treatment to the poor. It has beds for up to 1,400 patients. This is one of the many free health programs she runs. In 2005, the president of India gave her the Padma Bhushan Award, one of the country's highest civilian honors.

$150

The amount of money Mazumdar-Shaw had in 1978

- She used it all to start Biocon.
- Banks wouldn't give her a loan because she was a young woman with no business experience.
- Investors didn't want to risk their money on biotechnology because they hadn't heard of it before.

7

Susan Wojcicki: Moving Google out of the Garage

Susan Wojcicki in 2014.

Susan Wojcicki is one of the most powerful women in technology. She was born in Santa Clara, California, in 1968. Her father was a physics professor at Stanford. Her mother was a journalism teacher. Raised to be independent, Wojcicki and her two sisters would run around the neighborhood selling fruit door-to-door.

During her senior year at Harvard, Wojcicki learned about computer science. She was hooked. In 1998, she rented out her garage to Sergey Brin and Larry Page. The two used the space to start a new company called Google.

Wojcicki joined Google as its 16th employee. She was their first marketing manager. With no budget, she came up with the idea of putting Google's search engine on other websites. She also changed

5

Number of children Susan Wojcicki has

- Wojcicki is passionate about giving paid leave to new parents.
- Google offers employees 18 weeks of paid leave. Most other companies range from no paid leave to 12 weeks at the most.
- The United States is the only developed country in the world that does not offer national paid leave to new mothers.

WOMEN IN THE TECH INDUSTRY

In 2018, women held only 26 percent of the computer-related jobs in the United States. It wasn't always that way. From the 1950s into the 1970s, there were more women in computers than men. Since the 1980s, society has discouraged women from studying technology. Some women in technology are harassed by their male peers. Schools and companies need to better prepare and support women for these roles.

the way Google uses ads. In 2018, Google earned $116 billion in advertising money.

In 2014, Wojcicki was named CEO of YouTube, a video streaming service owned by Google. She has helped YouTube stars engage with their audiences. She also started YouTube's gaming and music channels.

8

Rosalind Brewer: A Self-Made Success

Rosalind Brewer was born in Detroit in 1962. Her parents taught her to work hard. They both worked long shifts at a General Motors (GM) plant.

Rosalind Brewer in 2016.

In 1984, Brewer graduated from Spelman College with a degree in chemistry. She became an organic chemist at Kimberly-Clark. But she was more interested in the business side of things. By 2004, she had worked her way up to global president of manufacturing.

Brewer moved to Walmart in 2006. She started out as a vice president of operations for the state of Georgia. In 2010, she was named president for the eastern United States. In this role, she oversaw 1,600 stores.

In 2012, Brewer became the first woman and the first African American CEO of Sam's Club, a Walmart company. She started several successful programs there, such as mobile checkout and curbside pickup.

In 2017, Brewer joined Starbucks as Chief Operating Officer (COO). Once more, she was the first woman and the first African American to hold this position.

9

Number of scholarships Rosalind Brewer established at Spelman College

- The scholarships are awarded to first-generation students. This means they are the first in their families to go to college.
- Brewer was a first-generation student when she attended Spelman.
- Brewer also leads mentorship circles at Spelman. These are groups of around 20 African American women who want to learn from her.

ARRESTS IN PHILADELPHIA

On April 12, 2018, two African American men entered a Starbucks in Philadelphia. They sat down to wait for a friend. After 10 minutes, the store manager called the police. People protested when a video of the men in handcuffs went viral. Rosalind Brewer was deeply saddened. She flew to Philadelphia with Starbucks CEO Kevin Johnson. They apologized. On May 29, 2018, they closed all Starbucks stores to educate employees on racism and racial bias.

9

Victoria Alonso: Creating Superheroes

23

Number of movies in the Marvel Cinematic Universe (as of 2019)

- The first film, *Iron Man*, was released in 2008.
- Marvel releases three films a year.
- The top-grossing MCU film as of 2019 is *Avengers: Endgame*, which has earned almost $3 billion worldwide.

As a young girl, Victoria Alonso loved going to the movies. She always stayed through the credits, hoping to see women's names. The only name she ever saw was Kathleen Kennedy, producer of *Star Wars*. Seeing that one name made Alonso think she could chase her own Hollywood dreams.

Alonso was born in 1965 in Buenos Aires, Argentina. At 19, she went to the University of Washington in Seattle to study drama. She wanted to be an actress. In 1990, she moved to Hollywood.

Alonso kept getting rejected as an actress. Then she was asked to work as a production assistant. As a lifelong lover of films, she accepted. She was soon doing production work for Oscar-nominated director Ridley

Some of the woman superheros from *Avengers: Endgame*.

Scott. She worked on the first *Shrek* movie.

In 2006, Alonso joined Marvel Studios as chief of visual effects. Her work made her an important part of the Marvel Universe. Fans wanted to see what she would do next to build the stories of Marvel superheroes.

Alonso was named executive vice president of physical production in 2015. This made her one of the top three people at Marvel. As a lesbian Latina, Alonso has been a strong advocate for different voices in the Marvel Universe. She's working on adding the first LBGTQ+ superhero. She is especially proud of *Black Panther* (2018) and *Captain Marvel* (2019).

THINK ABOUT IT

Victoria Alonso believes people want to see the superheroes they try to be in their own lives. Do you agree? What kind of superhero would you like to be? What would you fight for?

10

Marillyn Hewson: Advancing Weapons Technology

In 2018, *Fortune* magazine called Marillyn Hewson the most powerful woman in the world. She was born in 1953 in Junction City, Kansas. Her father died when she was nine. Her mother raised her and her four siblings. Hewson credits her mother for teaching her leadership and independence. All the kids had to pitch in on chores, bills, and grocery runs.

Marillyn Hewson in 2012.

Hewson worked nights to put herself through college. She graduated from the University of Alabama with a degree in business in 1977. In 1979, she earned her master's degree in economics. Her first job out of school was at the US Bureau of Labor Statistics.

In 1983, Hewson joined Lockheed Corporation as a senior industrial engineer. Lockheed (now called Lockheed Martin) designs defense and space technologies, mostly for the US government. Hewson's strong work ethic and dedication helped her rise to the top of the company. She has moved through 20 different positions during her time there.

In 2013, Hewson became Lockheed Martin's Chairman, President, and

The F-35A Lighting II fighter jet.

CEO. In this role, she has expanded the company's space program. She also oversaw completion of the F-35 fighter jet.

THINK ABOUT IT

Lockheed Martin works on technologies that take people out of weapons delivery. One example is a pilotless helicopter. This could save lives. But some people are protesting it. Why might they be against it?

$89.2 million

Cost of one F-35A Lighting II fighter jet

- The F-35A Lighting II is the world's most advanced fighter plane. It can move at 1.6 times the speed of sound.
- Sensors in the pilot's helmet allow them to see underneath the jet.
- The jet is used by militaries in 13 countries, including the United States.

11

Folorunsho Alakija: Leading with Faith

Folorunsho Alakija in 2013.

Folorunsho Alakija credits God for her successes in banking, fashion, and oil. She was born in Nigeria in 1951. Her father came from a long line of chiefs. This made him wealthy. He had eight wives and 52 children. This is acceptable for his religion and culture.

At seven, Alakija went to Wales to study. When she returned, she joined a bank as a secretary. She moved up to become the bank's first head of corporate affairs. In 1984, she quit her job to pursue her love of fashion. She returned to the United Kingdom and studied fashion in London. Her clothing line became very popular.

Alakija's fashion connections helped her secure an oil plot. In 1993, she started Famfa Oil Limited. She worked with oil giant Texaco to drill her plot. She became a billionaire.

Alakija believes that God has called her to help widows and orphans. They are not treated well in Nigeria. Through her Rose of Sharon Foundation, Alakija offers scholarships and microcredit opportunities to these families.

1986

Year when Folorunsho Alakija was named Nigeria's Fashion Designer of the Year

- She believes that God told her in a dream to name her clothing line Rose of Sharon House of Fashion.
- Her interest in fashion began when she was a child, helping in her mother's fabric shop.
- Alakija is a member of the Fashion Designers Association of Nigeria.

MICROCREDIT

Microcredit means giving very small loans at low interest rates to low-income borrowers. These are people who can't get loans from regular banks. A banker named Muhammad Yunus came up with the idea. He started the microcredit Grameen Bank in Bangladesh in 1976. Most of its loans went to groups of women. In 2006, Yunus and the bank won the Nobel Peace Prize.

In 2018, The Rose of Sharon Foundation celebrated its 10-year anniversary of helping widows and children.

12

Mary Kay Ash: Building a Beauty Empire

At 45, Mary Kay Ash was ready to retire. After 25 years in sales, she was tired of seeing less-qualified men getting the promotions she deserved. She started writing a book for women in business. She soon realized she was writing a plan for her own business. This was the beginning of Mary Kay Inc.

Ash was born in Hot Wells, Texas, in 1918. Her mother ran a café. Starting when she was seven years old, Ash took care of the home and her bedridden father. She realized early on that she had a talent for sales. She was the top cookie seller in her Girl Scout troop. She won prizes at school for her speeches.

Ash married at 17. She had three children. She sold books door-to-door to help with expenses. Then her husband left the family. Ash had to provide for her children on her own. She started working for Stanley Home Products. She sold their products out of her home. Ash worked for these types of sales companies, moving up through their ranks, until 1963. That was the year she started Mary Kay Inc.

Mary Kay Ash.

Top sales associates who earned pink Cadillacs arranged them in a giant 50 at their headquarters for the 50th anniversary of Mary Kay Inc. in 2013.

Both Ash's lawyer and her accountant thought her company would be a failure. She quickly proved them wrong. In the first year, Ash turned the $5,500 she used to start her skin care company into $198,000 worth of sales.

Ash passed away in 2001. But her company lives on. In 2018, Mary Kay Inc. produced over $3.5 billion in sales in nearly 40 countries.

13
Mary Kay Ash's lucky number

- Ash started Beauty by Mary Kay on September 13, 1963.
- The Mary Kay World Headquarters is 13 stories tall and has 13 elevators.
- The former office of Mary Kay Ash is on the 13th floor. It has not changed since her death in 2001.

Out of the Shadows

Eliza Lucas Pinckney

Pinckney was only a teenager when her father left the family in 1739. She took charge of his South Carolinian plantations. She experimented with indigo seeds. After three years, she figured out how to make indigo dye. She marketed the plant. By 1754, indigo was one of South Carolina's highest-selling crops.

Bridget "Biddy" Mason

Mason was born enslaved in 1818. In 1851, her slaveholder moved her to California, a free state. She sued for her freedom and won. She bought a piece of land that is now in Los Angeles. By investing in real estate, she earned almost $300,000, a fortune for that time.

Bridget "Biddy" Mason.

Rebecca Pennock Lukens

Lukens had five children and another on the way when her husband died. This required her to take over his iron business in 1825. She built the company up. She made business deals with major railroads and steamboat suppliers. The Lukens Steel Company existed in some form until 1998.

Olive Ann Beech

Beech founded the Beech Aircraft Company with her husband in 1932. The company developed military aircraft. She ran the company during its growth in World War II. After her husband's death in 1950, Beech ran the company for 18 more years. She expanded the company into space exploration and drone technology.

Olive Ann Beech, circa 1940.

Glossary

bankruptcy
When a person or company is unable to pay their bills. In business, this falls under the legal system. The courts may take property from the person or company.

bias
An opinion of someone or something that shows prejudice.

biotechnology
Using science to change natural organisms or chemicals to make a new product.

e-commerce
Buying or selling on the internet.

economy
The way a country or region creates and spends its money—through production, trade, and other means.

empire
A large group of businesses, usually spread throughout the world, that are controlled by one main business.

entrepreneur
Someone who starts and runs a business.

executive
Someone who manages or directs others.

interest
The money a borrower pays to use a lender's money. People pay interest on loans and things they buy on credit.

investors
People who put their own money into a company or product. They expect to make a future profit.

loans
Funds given with the expectation they will be repaid.

marketing
The way a product or service is promoted, especially through advertising.

Read More

Ellison, Katherine, and Ronnie Cohen. *Girl CEO: Fearless Advice from Trailblazing Women*. New York: Downtown Bookworks Inc., 2018.

Kapp, Diana. *Girls Who Run the World: 31 CEOS Who Mean Business*. New York: Delacorte Press, 2019.

Lusted, Marcia Amidon. *The Most Influential Women in Business*. Breaking the Glass Ceiling: The Most Influential Women. New York: Rosen Publishing Group, 2019.

Maggs, Sam, Ruth Amos, and Emma Grange. *Marvel Fearless and Fantastic! Female Super Heroes Save the World*. New York: DK Children, 2018.

White, Arisa, and Laura Atkins. *Biddy Mason Speaks Up*. Fighting for Justice. Berkeley, CA: Heyday Books, 2019.

Index

About the Author

Brianna L. DeVore has a bachelor's degree in women's studies and works in the publishing industry. She lives in Minnesota with her husband, cat, and two dogs.